THE PEOPLE OF GOD
IN THE OLD TESTAMENT

WORLD
CHRISTIAN
BOOKS

THE PEOPLE
OF GOD IN THE
OLD TESTAMENT

by H. J. KRAUS

ASSOCIATION PRESS, NEW YORK

THE PEOPLE OF GOD IN THE OLD TESTAMENT

———————

Copyright © 1958 by
H. J. Kraus

———————

Association Press, 291 Broadway, New York 7, N. Y.

The series *World Christian Books* is sponsored by
the International Missionary Council in co-opera-
tion with the Christian Literature Council of Great
Britain and the Committee on World Literacy and
Christian Literature of the United States. This
volume, under the same title, is published in
Great Britain by the United Society for Christian Literature (Lutterworth Press, London), 1958.
The Scripture quotations in this book are from
the Revised Standard Version of the Bible.

Price, $1.25

Library of Congress catalog card number: 58-11537

◄░░░►55

Printed in the United States of America
American Book–Stratford Press, Inc., New York

ABOUT WORLD CHRISTIAN BOOKS

TODAY it is not enough to believe; it is necessary also to understand. From every part of the world comes the demand for books that will help the Christian to understand his faith, to find the answers to the questions that he and other men are asking, and to know how to present the faith to others. The series WORLD CHRISTIAN BOOKS is planned to help in this particular area of Christian need. The books are directed in the first place to the "younger churches," but the old distinction between younger and older churches no longer really holds. All churches are faced by the same problems. In all countries the same questions are being asked. The series is specially planned for those who are called to preach and teach, in the hope that the materials given in these books may help them to carry out their task more effectively. But the aim has also been to write so simply that ordinary members of the church who wish to study their faith may be able to use these books as individuals or in study groups and so to grow in knowledge and understanding.

The books are being published first in English, but it is intended that as soon as possible they should be made available in the main languages of the Christian world. Writers have been chosen from various countries and various branches of the church, with special emphasis on the younger churches. This means that there will be a variety of voices, but the aim and the hope is that through many minds and many tongues the faith of the church in its one Lord may be clearly set forth.

STEPHEN NEILL
General Editor

Contents

Contents

Introduction

THE OLD TESTAMENT relates for us a very remarkable story. God, it tells us, has of his own free grace
directed his special attention to one small people—a
people of no particular importance in the great general
history of the world. This people God has called, chosen,
delivered, and endowed with many gifts of his favor and
of his presence. But this people he has also judged and
smitten more than any other people upon earth. The
prophet Amos, speaking in the name of God, makes the
following declaration: "You only have I known of all the
families of the earth; therefore I will punish you for all
your iniquities" (Amos 3:2). A profound mystery con-
trols the history of this chosen people Israel. In its midst
God has wrought those mighty works which point forward
to the coming of Jesus Christ, and at every stage proclaim that great event, the accomplishment of which is
recorded in the New Testament.

It is the aim of the present study, which deals with
the people of God in the Old Testament, to grasp and to
set forth some of the principal themes of the message of
the Old Testament. This can be done successfully only if
the historical background of this proclamation, made in

many and varied forms, is constantly borne in mind and referred to. Israel is no imaginary people; it is a real community, living in our world. God's revelation has really broken in on human history. It does not hang in the air, lifted high above the human realm of history and of this world. So it is impossible that this study should be carried out without constant reference back to that historical context within which the life of Israel was lived out. Yet we are not attempting to write, even in outline, a historical and critical "history of Israel." Our concern here is simply with that special message, in the light of which we are trying to understand the life of the people of God under the Old Covenant. We cannot, therefore, attempt for example a detailed reconstruction of the earliest phases of the history of Israel. Here it must suffice us to learn the principal themes of that proclamation, in which Israel set forth its own understanding of its earlier history. Only in particular cases are questions of history, chronology, and geography dealt with. The reader is recommended, if possible, to have by him a *History of Israel,* in order to acquaint himself more fully with the historical problems that underlie this study.

Above all, the writer would most strongly urge that each chapter of the present study should be carefully checked and tested by reference to the text of the Bible itself. The biblical references are of the utmost importance for the understanding of the whole context in which "the people of God in the Old Testament" moves.

chapter **1**

The Fellowship of the
Twelve Tribes

THE STARTING POINT of our study is a very important narrative in which we are given an account of the constitution of Israel as an alliance of twelve tribes. This narrative is to be found in the 24th chapter of the Book of Joshua.

On the initiative of Joshua, so we are told, the twelve tribes of Israel are gathered in Shechem (24:1). In his speech to the great assembly, Joshua begins with a backward glance at the earlier history of the various groups and tribes that are now gathered together at Shechem. Their forefathers used to live on the far side of the river Euphrates, and there they served other gods. And ever and again these groups and tribes are still inclined to offer allegiance to alien gods and powers. God has done great and mighty deeds in order to bring to his side those who are here addressed; and yet even now they still need a vigorous summons to obedience. Joshua cries aloud: "Now therefore fear the LORD, and serve him in sincerity and in faithfulness; put away the gods which your fathers served beyond the River, and in Egypt, and serve the

LORD. And if you be unwilling to serve the LORD, choose this day whom you will serve, whether the gods your fathers served in the region beyond the River, or the gods of the Amorites in whose land you dwell; but as for me and my house, we will serve the LORD" (Josh. 24:14–15). In answer to this challenge, all the twelve tribes affirm that they will serve the LORD alone, and that they will renounce allegiance to all alien gods (Josh. 24:16–18).

It is important to note that it is Joshua, together with his house, the house of Joseph (i.e., Ephraim and Manasseh), who takes the initiative in summoning the assembly, and in calling forth from the twelve tribes the common confession of their faith. In a decisive act all the assembled throng together declares that "it is the LORD our God who brought us and our fathers up from the land of Egypt" (vs. 17), that "we will serve the LORD" (vs. 21), and that "his voice we will obey" (vs. 24). On the basis of this confession, this solemn declaration, the twelve tribes enter into a covenant: "Joshua made a covenant with the people" (better: "brought the people into a covenant fellowship") "that day, and made statutes and ordinances for them at Shechem" (vs. 25). So, on the soil of the land of Canaan, the twelve tribes enter into a fellowship, which bears the name of Israel.

Israel is an association of tribes, which has accepted as the basis of its common life the worship of the LORD alone, and which has made a covenant to that effect. These words provide us with a fundamental and very significant definition of the meaning of the words, "the people of God in the Old Testament."

The meeting place of the tribes was a central sanctuary. In Joshua 24, the sanctuary of Shechem, which lay within

12

the territory of the "House of Joseph," is mentioned as the central place of worship. The distinguishing marks of the sanctuary at Shechem were an oak and a great stone (Josh. 24:26). At a later time the Ark of the Covenant came to be recognized as the sign of the presence of God among his people; this provided a second meeting place of the fellowship of the tribes. At other times the "holy tent," the tabernacle, and later still the Temple, served as the central sanctuary. We find also such places as Shiloh (1 Sam. 1:3), Bethel (Judg. 20:26), and Gilgal (Josh. 4:19–20) referred to as places of general assembly for the fellowship of the tribes of Israel. *The unity of the associated tribes was thus made manifest from time to time in meetings at the central sanctuaries.*

This organization of the life of a people in the form of an association of tribes is by no means unique. Other peoples in the neighborhood of Israel also organized themselves in the form of a confederation of tribes; and surprisingly enough, in these also twelve was the number at which the limit of the confederation was regularly fixed (Gen. 22:20–24; 25:13–16; 36:10–14). What we are dealing with, then, is a regular system, a manner of life with its own fixed laws, which goes back to the time before the formation of nations and of states. In the organization of life in this prepolitical era religion and worship played the most important part. But the fellowship of tribes acted, as far as possible, together and unanimously in its political affairs as well. Considering the parallels in the Bible record and beyond it, we may conclude that *Israel, as a fellowship of tribes with a central sanctuary, had adopted a form of life well adapted to the conditions which prevailed in the prepolitical period in the ancient world.*

In the twelfth century B.C. the confederation of the twelve tribes came into being in Palestine. But more important than the *form* of the organization of a people in the period before "states" came into being is the significance, the inner *meaning* of that which is represented by the fellowship of the twelve tribes. Let us take the name of the confederation as our starting point. It is called "Israel." And "Israel" means "God rules," or "God will rule." (Another, and rather different, explanation of the name Israel is given in Gen. 32:28.) One thing is certain: What gives to the assembly of the tribes at the central sanctuary the reality of its being and its particular value is the fact that the LORD is its Ruler. What is demanded of the people in response to this fundamental truth is service and obedience. In the central sanctuary, in the midst of Israel, the LORD is present as Ruler; this is the mystery and the marvel of the people of God in the Old Testament. In the poetic utterances of Balaam this mystery and marvel of Israel, and of its divine Ruler who is ever present in its midst, is set forth in two splendid verses, which we quote here without reference to their context:

> *lo, a people dwelling alone,*
> *and not reckoning itself among the nations!*

(Numbers 23:9)

> *He has not beheld misfortune in Jacob;*
> *nor has he seen trouble in Israel.*
> *The LORD their God is with them,*
> *and the shout of a king is among them.*

(Numbers 23:21)

It may well be that other divinities and powers dwell in the midst of other fellowships of tribes and determine the life of those confederations. In Israel, God alone is the Ruler. What that means will be more exactly explained later on. Our immediate concern must be to define more exactly in two directions the explanations that have already been given.

1. We shall not correctly understand the special character of Israel as a fellowship of tribes if we apply to it the standards implied in the generally accepted meaning of the word "people"; if, that is to say, we try to identify the natural, inherent powers, and the phenomena of growth and development that are present in Israel. The term "people" is generally taken to refer to a natural phenomenon. But the fellowship of the tribes has quite plainly come into existence as a historical entity in a specific historical situation. Its coming into being is due to the working of certain forces of historical destiny, such as the Old Testament could think of as "manifestations of the guidance of God."

As we can plainly see from Joshua 24, Israel is called, invited, and challenged to the service of the one God, who dwells in the midst of the fellowship of the tribes. What we are dealing with here is a decision, and a confession of faith. It is impossible here to think in terms of a natural process of development. Even if we go further back, to consider the earlier existence of one particular tribe or another, we shall still in the end come back to some historical cause. Even the tribe is not a natural entity; it is an entity which has come into being as a result of certain historical conditions. In the process of entering into the land of Canaan the tribes had shared a common destiny, and this had helped forward their development as tribes. In consequence, we must not understand the word "people" in the Old Testament as though it described a phenomenon of natural growth; we must always take it in the sense of "a fellowship which has come into being in history and for historical reasons." The creative power, however, that dwells in Israel is the word of God the Ruler, that word which calls, and delivers, and gathers into one.

2. There is a natural and recurrent tendency to apply to the organization of the twelve tribes the term "theocracy," the direct rule of God. This term doubtless refers to something that is genuinely important; it hits off accurately one element in the ordering of Israel's life. The intention of those who use it is to find a term which corresponds to the fact that God rules, that he stands alone at the very center of the life of the fellowship. But the word "theocracy" is heavily charged with associations that are out of place here. It calls up the picture of an organized state; a state that has been founded on a religious basis through the power of a priesthood, and that *consciously* organizes the whole of its life on the basis of the divine authority. But in the fellowship of the twelve tribes we find no trace of this deliberate plan of organization, of this capacity deliberately to create institutions for the ordering of the people's life.

The sovereignty of God in the life of the alliance of the twelve tribes is an event, a continuing *activity* of God; it is not a *principle* that can be used as the basis for the organization of a state. It is a power which breaks forth upon the life of the people, which works outward from the very center of its being. Such a power can never

16

be brought within the limits of an institution directed by an order of priests. The truth that God rules in Israel is a truth that is proclaimed as ever new; it is not set forth, in fixed and unchangeable form, in the institutions in which the life of the people is organized.

On the one side is the understanding of "a people" in terms of natural growth and development. On the other side is the "theocracy," a rule of God expressing itself in fixed and permanent institutions. The special character of the life of Israel can become clear only when we have grasped the difference between it and these other two forms of national life. This is of basic importance for the more detailed studies that will follow.

chapter 2

The Proclamation of Israel's Origins

WHEN THE CONFEDERATION of the twelve tribes gave account of the events through which it had come into being and of its own earlier history, it did not do so in the style of a historical narrative of events that had taken place solely within the confines of this world. What Israel did was to recall and to proclaim *the mighty deeds of God,* that God to whom Israel owed its very being. And this corresponded to the facts. The fellowship of the twelve tribes had not come into being through the mighty breaking out of a people bent on the accomplishment of its own aims, a people that overcame all resistance by its own power, that carried on war with its own resources, and so entered into possession of a land that was not its own. On the contrary; it was God who had taken hold of the life of wandering groups of nomads, had opened the way before the forefathers of Israel, and had given them the land of Canaan as a gift. So what the fellowship of the tribes had to set forth was not the history of a way that it had followed independently and on its own initiative. It could only point again and again to the way in which

18

God had met the ancestors of Israel, called them, delivered them, and led them on to the accomplishment of his own good purposes.

The forefathers of the fellowship of the tribes had been caught up into a great and mighty act of God. Israel's history is a history of salvation; a history in which and through which God brings help and salvation into the world. The three great groups of subjects in which this history of salvation are set forth are the following: (1) The Deliverance from Egypt; (2) The Revelation of God, the Covenant, and the communication of the Law of God at Sinai; (3) The Promises made to the patriarchs.

Before we direct our attention to these three great groups of subjects, we ought first to answer the question — when? On what occasions did the fellowship of the twelve tribes recall to memory the circumstances of its origin, and at the same time the great saving acts of God that were the foundation of its being?

The fellowship of the twelve tribes of Israel met three times a year for the great festivals in the central sanctuary. It was laid down (Exod. 23:14) that the whole people of Israel should appear before the LORD at Passover in spring, at the Feast of Weeks in the middle of summer, and at the Feast of Tabernacles in the autumn. On these occasions of worship the assembled throng was assured once again of the God-given foundation of its life. The heart of the feast of the Passover was the story of the deliverance of the people from Egypt; Tabernacles recalled the events of the self-revelation of God at Sinai, the making of the Covenant, and the giving of the Law.

1. The deliverance from Egypt is, then, the principal theme of the feast of the Passover, the great event that

is commemorated in it. In the Christian Churches, Good Friday and Easter are above all else festivals in which the message of the crucifixion and the resurrection of Jesus Christ is set forth. In exactly the same way, the deliverance of Israel from Egypt was the center and the climax of the proclamation that was made at the time of the feast of the Passover.

From Exodus 12 we learn that the feast of the Passover was celebrated in the family circle. The Passover lamb was slain, and then the thoughts of all turned to the great theme drawn from the history of salvation. It seems that there was an older form of the celebration of the Passover feast, in which the whole fellowship of the tribes took part (Josh. 5:10–12). However that may be, there were always three elements in the observance of the day of the feast. First, the mighty works of God were recounted. The tale was told how God, through terrible plagues and mighty manifestations of his power, had delivered the oppressed Israelites from the powerful hand of Pharaoh. Then the events that had taken place on the night of the deliverance were repeated in dramatic and contemporary form (Exod. 12:11). Finally, the incomparable event that followed upon the act of God was celebrated in a song of praise. The great hymn of the Passover rings out:

> *I will sing to the* LORD, *for he has triumphed gloriously;*
> *the horse and his rider he has thrown into the sea.*
> *The* LORD *is my strength and my song,*
> *and he has become my salvation;*
> *this is my God, and I will praise him,*
> *my father's God, and I will exalt him.*

20

Who is like thee, majestic in holiness,
terrible in glorious deeds, doing wonders?

(Exodus 15:1, 2, 11)

The proclamation made at the feast of the Passover is the central message of the whole Old Testament. The deliverance from Egypt is the beginning and the crucial point of the whole history of salvation. God has here made plain the direction in which his will and his acts are moving. He has mightily entered into the movement of history. He has taken hold of a group of helpless slaves, has himself made for them a way into freedom, and has given them a new basis for their existence. The mystery and the marvel of God's care for his people, of his choice of them for himself, are present implicitly in the proclamation made at the feast of the Passover. It is in the light of these events that Israel understands its own existence. Thus the proclamation is made to the fellowship of the twelve tribes: "For you are a people holy to the LORD your God; the LORD your God has chosen you to be a people for his own possession, out of all the peoples that are on the face of the earth. It was not because you were more in number than any other people that the LORD set his love upon you and chose you, for you were the fewest of all peoples; but it is because the LORD loves you, and is keeping the oath which he swore to your fathers, that the LORD has brought you out with a mighty hand, and redeemed you from the house of bondage, from the hand of Pharaoh king of Egypt" (Deut. 7:6–8). This makes it impossible for Israel to claim any merit or excellence of his own. The LORD has loved and chosen Israel —this fact alone comes into consideration as an adequate

21

basis for the special existence of this fellowship. Furthermore, the LORD cares for the insignificant, and comes down to the level of the lost and of the prisoners. Here already in the Old Testament we hear the accents of the New Testament gospel, with its total freedom from illusions about the people of God.

2. The self-disclosure of God at Sinai, and with it the making of the covenant and the communication of the law of God, is the central theme, the special significance, of the Feast of Tabernacles—in particular once every seven years. In the regulations for the feasts which we find in the Book of Deuteronomy we read as follows: "At the end of every seven years, at the set time of the year of release, at the feast of booths, when all Israel comes to appear before the LORD your God at the place which he will choose, you shall read this law before all Israel in their hearing" (Deut. 31:10–11).

We can best picture to ourselves the way in which this solemn act was carried out if we read carefully Deuteronomy 27:11–26. This tells how the twelve tribes come together at Shechem, on the slopes of Mount Ebal and Mount Gerizim. The Levites begin to speak, and proclaim the law of God before the assembled congregation. From these indications in the Old Testament, and from a number of scattered observations, it is possible to conclude that the events which are recorded for us in Joshua 24, and which we used as the introduction to our first chapter, did not take place only once, but were repeated again and again in a solemn act of worship. At the central sanctuary the confederation of the twelve tribes was ever and again called back to its covenant relationship with the LORD, and pledged anew to

22

the service of God through obedience to his law. So those things which happened at Sinai are not simply a series of historical happenings in the past; in the solemn worship of the twelve tribes they become again a present and contemporary reality. This is expressly set forth in Deuteronomy 5:2–3: "The LORD our God made a covenant with us in Horeb. Not with our fathers did the LORD make this covenant, but with us, who are all of us here alive this day." In these words the peculiar character of the proclamation of history in the Old Testament is made plain to us. The history of salvation deals with events which have really taken place in the past; but the events have been transformed into a reality of salvation which is significant and vital even today. In the solemn worship of the twelve tribes the mighty acts of God in the past become an immediately present reality. The word of proclamation makes visible the basis of Israel's being. Unless this word is spoken, the fellowship of the twelve tribes is in danger of falling away into the error of self-assertion and self-determination.

"I am the LORD your God" (Exod. 20:2). This declaration at the beginning of the Decalogue contains the whole mystery and wonder of that revelation of God, which was first given at Sinai, and was renewed again and again in the liturgy of the feast. God makes himself known, and pronounces his name. JHVH is the name of the God of the Old Covenant.* This name of God must be understood strictly as a personal name, and we are

---

* In the Hebrew text of the Old Testament this sacred Name of God is written without the vowels, as we have written it here. In the Revised Standard Version it is generally represented by "LORD" in capitals, and this is the usage that has been followed in most places in this book.

not supposed to ask what it may mean. We do find in Exodus 3:14 an interpretation of the name; this is based on the fact that this divine name does look rather as though it was connected with the Hebrew verb "to be." From this similarity was derived the interpretation of the name as "being." But the nature of God is not to be understood as "abstract being"; it is always "being in relation to someone." God declares himself to be the God who is, and who will be, *for Israel*. And, though his manifestation takes place to the accompaniment of the terror of fire, the quaking of the mountain, and the thunders of heaven, his coming in this way is not a sign of hostility to Israel. "I am thy God." That is the decisive word to Israel. In his majesty and his holiness the almighty LORD is there on Israel's behalf as Israel's God. This quite definite relationship between the God who has come forth from his hiddenness and the people of whom his mighty word has taken hold finds its expression in the making of the covenant. The confederation of the twelve tribes enters into a covenant relationship with God, which is to be the determining factor in its existence, and within which the whole of its life is to be lived. What happened long ago at Sinai is once again repeated in the liturgy; to the listening throng the summons once again goes forth: "This day you have become the people of the LORD your God" (Deut. 27:9).

The creative word of God brings into existence a new reality: the people of God. Where God is present in his covenant, there he reveals himself as Lord in mighty acts and miracles before the eyes of all the peoples of the earth (Exod. 34:10). But it is in the first place over Israel that his lordship is exercised: "I am the LORD your

24

God, who brought you out of the land of Egypt, out of the house of bondage. You shall have no other gods before me" (Exod. 20:2–3). In Israel, within the closed circle of the covenant, the LORD wills to be the sole Lord of all life. That is what the Old Testament is all about. The people whom the LORD has freed has become the people of God. From this point on no other deity can make claim to any authority over them. When God demands the obedience of the twelve tribes, this is no arbitrary demand; it is based on the covenant in which he has declared Israel to be his own possession. Thus it is only in relation to the covenant that the significance of the commandments of God can be fully understood: "Keep silence and hear, O Israel: this day you have become the people of the LORD your God. You shall *therefore* obey the voice of the LORD your God, keeping his commandments and his statutes, which I command you this day" (Deut. 27:9–10). *The happenings at Sinai, especially the direct utterance of God to his people and his claim upon them, are brought back to the memory of Israel in the liturgy of the feast as that event upon which the life of the people rests, and by which its character is determined.*

3. Having considered the two great themes of the feasts of Passover and Tabernacles, we must now turn to the stories of the patriarchs. And here the proclamation of the history reaches far back, to the very first beginning of the earliest history of Israel. The patriarchs came from the eastern world. Ur of the Chaldeans (Gen. 11:28) and Haran (Gen. 11:31) are mentioned as their earlier homes. They wandered from place to place. They had no settled dwelling. They were looking for a country. As nomadic shepherds they passed from place to place,

25

pitched their tents for a time, and then moved on. They could accumulate considerable wealth (Gen. 13:2), but they never found a place of rest.

When the patriarchs first moved in the direction of Palestine, the land was still firmly in the possession of its original inhabitants. Abraham, Isaac, and Jacob could dwell only as "strangers and sojourners" in the "Sown Land." They lived at peace with the regular dwellers in the land, and entered into serious rivalry only with other groups which, like themselves, were driven onward by land hunger (Gen. 13:7). That is the outward picture which a study of the narratives of the patriarchs reveals to us. But Israel was never much interested in the outward aspects of the life of its forefathers; its interest lay elsewhere— in that divine summons from another world, of which the patriarchs had become aware.

Abraham was the first to hear the call of God: "Go from your country and your kindred and your father's house to the land that I will show you. And I will make of you a great nation, and I will bless you . . . and in you all the families of the earth will be blessed" (Gen. 12:1-3). In this word of God to Abraham is to be found the master clue to the understanding of the whole of Old Testament history. The starting point of the history of man's salvation is God's call to man and nothing else. This call involves separation from all other peoples of the earth. It was not natural inner powers, or the coming together of favorable historical circumstances, or ideas and programs, or human purposes and decisions, that called Israel into being; it was the word of God alone. This call, with its trenchant demand for separation, is at the same time promise. Out of Abraham a great people will grow,

26

and this people will be the bearer of blessing to all peoples. *By way of Abraham and Israel God enters into the world of the nations.* The whole Old Testament message is based on the first call and on the first promise, of which Abraham was the recipient. But the sound of this call does not die away. Abraham is not left alone. The stories of the patriarchs tell us that God led Abraham and was always with him. This idea of the presence of God as guide is the determining factor in the narratives. The history of the people of God from its earliest beginnings is the history of a unique guidance, which is made possible only through the presence of God with his people. It is accompanied by ever fresh promises, directing the eyes of men toward the future, revealing the future to them. Thus, the land of Canaan is promised to the patriarchs as the goal of their wanderings—that land through which they were then passing as "strangers and sojourners." Their descendants would win this land and take possession of it as their own. This was the great word that pointed to the future; it was the fulfillment of this word in later times that gave to the patriarchs their immense significance for the life of Israel.

In the confederacy of the twelve tribes of Israel the stories of the patriarchs were told and retold, and were accepted as revealing at one and the same time the deepest foundation of the existence of the people, its generally accepted principles, and the inspiration of its life.

chapter **3**

Judges, Saviors, and Kings

THE LORDSHIP of God, as set forth in the law and
the commandments, was the central point of the life of the
confederation of the twelve tribes of Israel. The LORD,
the God of Israel, manifests himself as the God of law.
As can be seen from the codes of law in the Old Testament, there were two types of law in Israel. There was
the "prophetic" law of God, in which principles were set
forth. There was also the law of everyday life, adminis-
tered by the priests, and applicable to human situations
in all their variety. Characteristic of the first type are the
Ten Commandments, with their prophetic and declaratory
summons: "Thou shalt . . . ." At the Feast of Tabernacles
this law of God was solemnly proclaimed. In contrast to
this, the second type was extended to cover all the changes
and chances of life, and provided an appropriate penalty
for every imaginable misdemeanor. By way of example
we may quote the following rule: "When men quarrel
and one strikes the other with a stone or with his fist and
the man does not die but keeps his bed, then if the man
rises again and walks abroad with his staff, he that struck

28

him shall be clear; only he shall pay for the loss of his time, and shall have him thoroughly healed" (Exod. 21:18–19). The administration of this kind of law was dealt with at the gate of the village. Here, under the direction of the elders of the place, plaintiff, witnesses, and defendants met together. But even in such a situation it is not a question of a legal decision in purely worldly terms; here too the principle is that the whole of life is determined by the law of God. This detailed law-giving too is permeated by the LORD's claim to sovereignty.

The highest responsible court of appeal in the confederation of the twelve tribes was the "Judge of Israel." In early times, in the so-called "period of the Judges," the judge was the central figure of the whole fellowship. Thus in the lists in Judges 10:1–5 and 12:7–15, we are given in unbroken succession the names of those men who "judged Israel." From Deuteronomy 17:8–9 we learn that in difficult cases those responsible for the administration of justice in the various settlements of the Israelites in the land could have recourse to the judge who exercised authority at the central sanctuary. He was the final court of appeal; on him rested the duty of responsibly expounding and applying the law of God. But this "Judge of Israel" could never establish a claim as *ruler* over the people. He was the administrator of the law of God and nothing else. "Political questions," in this prepolitical era of the fellowship of the tribes, were dealt with in the council of the spokesmen of the tribes and the elders.

How was the fellowship of the tribes to act when its existence was threatened by hostile attack? In the ancient world, war was not simply a secular or political affair; it had something to do with religion too. So, in Israel, war like everything else was brought into relation to the principle of the sovereignty of God.

The following outline can be given of the outward procedure that was to be followed when Israel had a "holy war" on its hands: The men of Israel are called out by the blast of the trumpet (Judg. 3:27; 6:34, etc.). The bands of warriors come together at the appointed meeting place (Judg. 5:14 f.). In a great armed camp "the people of the LORD" equips itself (Judg. 5:11, 13; 20:2) for its warlike enterprise. Strict rules of dedication and of purity must be observed (Josh. 3:5; 1 Sam. 21:6). Sacrifices are offered (1 Sam. 7:9). Through the prophets inquiry is made as to whether God approves the enterprise (Judg. 20:23).

If the answer is given in the name of God that "truly the LORD has given all the land into our hands" (Josh. 2:24), the whole host is assured that the LORD himself goes before (Judg. 4:14) to deliver his people in their need. The wars of Israel are the wars of God (1 Sam. 18:17).

In these holy wars, however, the focus of the whole affair is the "deliverer" whom God has sent and endued with the Spirit of the LORD. The deliverer of Israel is designated as such by a prophet (Judg. 4:6) or by a special personal call (Judg. 6:11 ff.). Gideon and Barak —to name only these two—are specially endowed leaders of Israel in war. The Spirit of God inspires them to do exploits. They are instruments of God, who brings about victory through their deeds. But, just as the "Judge of Israel" was only the highest legal authority and no more, so the specially endowed "deliverers" served as leaders only for the duration of the holy war. No question of a claim to permanent authority could arise. The union of the tribes is not a political association; it is an association based on the worship of God.

But it was just at this point that differences of opinion inevitably arose. How could such a union of tribes, based on the worship of God, be adequate to meet the bitter opposition with which it was faced in Palestine? The invasion of the so-called "Sea-faring Peoples," above all that of the Philistines, had to be met by a more stable ordering of society than could be provided by the liturgical fellowship of the tribes. In quite early times we can detect in Israel a tendency to make permanent the authority of the deliverer, whom God had called and appointed and endued with the free, untransferable gift of his grace. So, for example, the elders of Israel come to Gideon with an urgent plea that he will allow himself to be made king, and will so prepare the way for a more settled organization of the life of the people (Judg. 8:22). The reply of Gideon to the elders is very significant: "I will not rule over you, and my son will not rule over you; the LORD will rule over you" (Judg. 8:23). Yet Gideon's refusal of the crown could not prevent other attempts being made to bring about further developments and a more stable organization of the fellowship of the tribes (Judg. 9).

In the time of Samuel, the distress of the tribes under the repeated attacks of the Philistines had reached a point at which the need for firm, central leadership had become clear beyond all possibility of denial. Saul, who began his career as a "specially endowed deliverer," was raised to the kingship by the acclamation of the people. But no sooner was this done than irreconcilable opposition manifested itself between the new institution of the kingship and the old liturgical ordering of the people's life. It could almost have been foreseen that Saul would bring disaster upon himself by his lack of respect for these ancient traditions and orders of worship (1 Sam. 13:8–14), and, further, by his attempt after the victory over the Amalekites to behave in the manner of an oriental potentate (1 Sam. 15:12). So here was posed the decisive question for the developing kingship, the question on which its very existence depended: Could it arrive at a satisfactory understanding with the ancient liturgical traditions of the fellowship of the twelve tribes?

When Saul failed, David succeeded. He accepted the liturgical institutions of the confederation of the twelve tribes as the foundation for his dynasty. When, as a young ruler in the area inhabited by the southern tribes, he had been recognized by those tribes as king, and when the northern tribes also had entered into negotiation with him, the new king of Israel captured Jerusalem, and appointed it to be not only the central royal residence between north and south, but, more important than all, to be also the central place of worship for the whole fellowship of the twelve tribes. The king of Israel linked his kingdom to the ancient traditions of the people. He brought up the Ark and the tabernacle of the LORD to Jerusalem, and accepted these symbols of the central sanctuary as the foundation on which his kingdom was to be built.

Nevertheless, the introduction of hereditary kingship into the life of Israel resulted in far-reaching changes. The prepolitical ordering of the life of the confederation of the tribes has been transformed into the organization of a state. The central sanctuary of the tribes has become the central sanctuary of a kingdom. Yet David held unswervingly to the principle of the sovereignty of God in Israel. *The human kingship is no more than a representation of the divine sovereignty*. It is only through the unconditional submission of each ruler in succession to the will of the LORD that the sovereignty of God over his people can continue to be a reality.

Already in the time of Solomon, the first to succeed to the throne of David, the kingship is faced with a situation of ominous perplexity. It has already become clear that the alliance between the national sanctuary and the royal authority presents a great many problems. For where, in future, is the decisive authority to be found? In the worship of God, and in the sovereignty of God that is there proclaimed—or in the kingship? Will the king allow himself to be guided by God and exercise his functions only as "the Elect of the LORD"? Or will the king misuse the authority that is his by virtue of his "election" and claim the right to order the worship of God independently and according to his own predilections? If the king once sets himself free from the sovereignty of God and carries out policies of his own devising, no longer inquiring after the will of the LORD, the whole people of God has lost that which makes it the people of God and constitutes its mission.

This is the supreme interest in the whole history of the kingship in Israel. The writers of the history regularly ask: What is the attitude of this new ruler to the sovereignty of God? Is he, with all his heart and with all his powers, subject to the word of God's sovereignty? Furthermore, in this historical account of the kingdom all the later kings can be measured against the standard of David: Do they behave as David did, or do they follow new ways of their own devising? *David serves as the model of a kingship which is based on the sovereignty of God, and is wholly devoted to the service of God.* Very few of the later rulers measure up to this standard. David towers over the later history in solitary grandeur as *the* king of Israel. The ideal from the past is then transformed into an ideal of the future, for which men yearn. The form of the kingship as it was in David's days was full of promise, but the hopes set on it were frustrated; so, throughout its entire history, Israel awaited a final fulfillment and accomplishment of the ideal. In this expectation the ideas of judge, deliverer, and king flow together in the single figure of the Mediator, who will serve as the link between the invisible God and that people which stands in need of the guidance of its God.

chapter **4**

Apostasy

THROUGH a unique series of mighty acts the LORD had chosen and called Israel to be the people of God. But was Israel qualified to take upon itself the responsibilities of a life in covenant relationship with God? The whole Old Testament answers this question with a decisive "No!" This people, called by God, elected and brought into a covenant relationship with him, was from the beginning inclined to reject its calling, to despise the election, and to break the covenant.

The narrative of the golden calf (Exod. 32) sets forth beyond the possibility of misunderstanding the nature of Israel's reaction to God's affirmation of his covenant with his people. Moses, the accredited mediator of the word of God's sovereignty, has been absent for little more than a moment when the people fall into a state of hopeless religious confusion. They wish to see that invisible God, who has called and delivered them out of Egypt, and to observe a festival in his honor. The image of a calf is made from their golden ornaments. This image was not intended to represent some strange God; it was to be the representation of the LORD, the God of Israel himself. The calf, the symbolic figure, which in the ancient world stood for overwhelming power and fertility, is intended to bring God near to the people. Israel will not allow the LORD to draw near to his people in his own free and uncontrolled power; they will not wait for the accredited mediator, who makes known to them the word of God's sovereignty. That people arrogantly undertakes to draw near to the LORD with its own ready-made picture of God, and to offer to him a worship that is derived from the surrounding world of the heathen religions. What they have done without realizing it has been to assimilate the LORD to the world of the heathen gods. Israel had the best intentions; its only purpose was to worship the LORD. And yet the covenant has been broken; for an alien power, an alien image, has broken its way into the circle of the life of the people of God. No solemn protestations are of any avail. Although they emphatically assert, "These are your gods, O Israel, who brought you up out of the land of Egypt!" (Exod. 32:4)—this god is a foreign body. The festivals of this god are not the festivals of the LORD, the God of Israel.

The LORD had done everything possible for his people; yet immediately after the conclusion of the covenant, Israel turned away to the worship of a strange god. Not for a single instant is the people whom God has called capable of remaining faithful to the LORD, of waiting for his word, and of trusting in him alone. John Calvin called the heart of man an idol-factory—a factory which is always at work, and which brings forth its most wonderful products within the covenant relationship with God! What this means is that when the highest religious values of *this* world are confused with the revelation that breaks in upon us from *God's* world, man brings forth the wonderful achievements of his idolatry. This is as clear as could be in the case of Israel. Nowhere does the Old Testament present us with the picture of a godly, obedient, and believing people. The heathen are faithful to their gods and to the powers that they worship. But Israel responds to the living God, the God who in his love has given to it the gifts of freedom and of life, with a decisive "No!" "We will not have him to rule over us!"

What, then, does Israel want? In 1 Samuel 8:5 we find the outspoken declaration: "We wish to be like the other nations." God's people, that is to say, does not wish to be the people of God. It wishes to adapt not merely its God but also itself to the ordinary conditions that prevail generally in this world. Human powers of leadership step in, in place of the sovereignty of God. The demand for a king is accompanied by the comment of the LORD: "They have rejected me from being king over them" (1 Sam. 8:7).

We have seen that David is an exception to this rule. It is his purpose that in his exercise of his royal sovereignty, the sovereignty of God should find expression. But most of the rulers of Israel exercise their office in independence of God. All their thoughts and all their actions are directed toward the establishment of a state that can exist in this political world, and that must therefore be guided by the laws and the ideas current in this world order. What are the word and the guidance of Jehovah good for in the world of the nations? In that world, is it not the business of each state to maintain its own independence in its own way?

When Solomon, the great splendor-loving ruler of the state of Israel, died, it became clear for the first time how deeply the life of the people of the twelve tribes had been penetrated by the habit of thinking only in terms of political aims. The unifying sovereignty of God proved unable to resist the challenge of political forces, which rent Israel in twain. The one fellowship of the tribes broke up into two states, of which one (Israel) kept the old honored traditional name and included the majority of the tribes; the other (Judah) had within it, as the most precious of its possessions, the last central sanctuary of Israel. From now on both states were dominated by a never-resting tension between the religious inheritance from the past and the new national, political, and dynastic ambitions.

Israel and Judah were both caught up in the ebb and flow of the currents of world history in the Middle East. Situated as they were between the massive powers of Assyria and Egypt, the two dwarf states tried to find a way to survive. According to the generally accepted rules of political action, an alliance with one or other of the great powers was the obvious solution. But what have such alliances to do with the people of God? (1) If the people of God comes to lean on the powers of this world and to trust in them, it has, in fact, rejected the helping and protecting hand of its own God. Worse still, Israel does not really believe that the LORD can himself maintain his position and carry out his purposes in the world of the nations. (2) The great powers of the ancient East also had their gods, who were believed to maintain and protect the existence of these states. If Israel turned to these states for help, that implied that Israel was putting its trust in the gods of these states. Moreover, in the ancient world every alliance had its religious aspect. Therefore, when the people of God made one of these partly political and partly religious alliances, it was breaking the covenant of its God and entering the sphere in which the gods of the heathen exercised authority. *Israel had come to the conclusion that, in the practical affairs of life, the idea of the sovereignty of God just did not work.*

We might suppose that the people of God had by some express declaration repudiated its allegiance to the LORD, that Israel had declared its covenant with the LORD to be at an end. But this is not in the least what happened. The people of God cannot get free from him. The word of election and the mighty acts of God's love have knit themselves too intimately about the very heart of Israel's life. There is only one way in which these basic, unforgotten happenings can be brought into line with more recent events—JHVH the sovereign LORD of Israel must be transformed into Israel's own national God. The election comes to be regarded as a privilege, which Israel of its own free choice has made its own; while the great basic saving acts of God are turned into a source of arrogant self-confidence. "To us, the people of God, no ill can happen." "We are safeguarded in all our ways." The LORD himself is dragged down to the depths of the people's fall. He is reduced to the level of a religious and political tool, an idol, by means of which Israel can ensure the success of its own undertakings. On one point all have long been in agreement—that God may no longer exercise sovereignty over them through his word. Israel has forgotten his Creator (Hos. 8:14).

The guilt of the people in the political realm is paralleled in the religious field by their ever-present inclination to take up with *the worship of the Canaanites*. The aboriginal population of Palestine, the so-called Canaanites, worshiped and offered sacrifices to the Baalim, the deities of the Sown Land. The Baal is the unseen, mysterious owner of a tract of land. On the high places, by the springs, in the whispering of the leaves of the trees, the power that rules in each area makes itself known. Man expects fertility and blessing as a gift from this power. He worships it on the high places, by the springs, and under the green trees. Who can escape falling under the spell of the local deities of the fertile land?

The Old Testament makes it plain that Israel in Palestine fell immediately under the spell of the heathen powers of nature. The Israelites, in addition to their visits to their own central sanctuary, went up to worship also in the high places of the Baalim. Must it not be right, they argued, to pray to the local deities, and to thank them for the good gifts of the land? So Israel moved in an uncertain rhythm between the worship of the LORD and the worship of the Baalim. How then could the word of the LORD, as the God who promises and who gives, make itself heard? How was it possible to comprehend that the land, with all its visible realities, that had been there before Israel ever entered it, was in truth "the land of JHVH"? The LORD was brought down to the level of the heathen powers of nature. He was worshiped as though he were one of the Baalim. Through this confusion of God with Baal the whole religious life of Israel was disfigured.

40

But it was not only in the realm of history and in the world of nature that the apostasy of Israel became manifest. The whole social order of the nation's life was thrown into confusion by alien influences. In earlier times great care had been taken to secure that the tribes, clans, and families should receive fair and equal shares in the land of Canaan. But later a perilous falling away from this principle was to be observed. The desire of the royal court for splendor and wealth left its deep traces on the life of Israel. External trade brought goods and treasures into the land, and as a result comfort and luxury increased. The old social order of the confederacy of the tribes broke down. The rich spread themselves abroad, thrust the poor out of their way, and controlled the destiny of both the kingdoms. The members of the influential circles in Israel exuded wealth and security. The guiding principle of their lives and actions was the consciousness of being the best people in what itself was a privileged people.

In this general apostasy of the people could the central sanctuary no longer make its authority felt? Had all the traditions of the confederacy of the twelve tribes completely disappeared both in the northern kingdom of Israel and in the southern kingdom of Judah? In the earliest period of Israel's history sacrifice had played only a limited part in the life of worship. The central point of the life of the confederation of the tribes had been the proclamation and the practice of the law of God. But in the worship of the sanctuary of Israel increasing importance came gradually to be attached to sacrifice. We have already seen how the sovereignty of God was rejected by Israel, under the impulse of new concepts in the fields of

41

politics, nature worship, and social order. We have observed the way in which the LORD was increasingly assimilated to the new demands of the people, how he was
transformed into a religious instrument, in fact into an
idol. In this steadily advancing corruption, the practice of
sacrifice could only be yet another weight to drag the faith
of Israel still further into the depths. The people aimed,
by means of its burnt offerings and meal offerings, at exercising influence on the LORD, at enticing him to follow
them in their ways, at disposing him in their favor, at
spreading a thick cloud over all their transgressions. They
approach God with a multitude of religious observances;
it is genuinely their intention to give him the best that
they have—but the net result of all this is to reduce the
LORD to silence. God is no longer the one who determines
what men are to be; he is to be what men determine him
to be. Sacrifice is the pious fog, in which in a queer way
we move far from God, always with the intention and
in the hope of making God our own.

*Nowhere is ungodliness so monstrous, guilt so deep,
and unbelief so desperate as in this pious fog, which the
people of God has produced in order, on the best religious
principles, to set itself free from the sovereignty of the*
LORD. Between the clear day of the radiant revelation of
God and the dark night of heathenism lies the eerie gloom
of this confusion between heaven and earth. Here mighty
storms are brewing, which will later discharge themselves
in the history of Israel. God's gracious sovereignty beats
against a dead wall of passionate refusal that makes use
of every possible means of religious observance to protect
itself against being found out and identified as ungodliness.
God is put to death—through political alliances, through

42

worship of the powers of nature, through riches, and through the pious offering of sacrifices. The shadow of the cross of Christ falls athwart the Old Testament: "We do not want this man to reign over us" (Luke 19:14).

chapter **5**

The Prophetic Word

AT THE END of the last chapter we asked whether there was no power, in or connected with the ancient sanctuaries of Israel, that could set itself in opposition to the general apostasy and to the process of disintegration that was spreading in all directions. We must now occupy ourselves with the answer to that question. There is another line of development in Old Testament religion besides that which we have been considering; that line is prophecy, and this is the next subject with which we must briefly deal.

The sovereignty of God and the law of God are nowhere so clearly recognizable in the Old Testament as in those "declaratory" laws, of which the Decalogue is the most notable. But the Ten Commandments themselves are recognizably prophetic in character. In them it is the LORD himself who speaks. Moses, as a prophet, transmits the words of God to the people. It is no accident that in certain passages of the Old Testament Moses is spoken of as a prophet. In Deuteronomy 18:15, for instance, there is an extremely important sentence, which literally

44

translated from the Hebrew runs as follows: "A prophet like unto me will JHVH our God *from time to time* cause to arise from the midst of your brethren—to him shall you listen!" A little later follows God's promise to Moses himself: "I will raise up for them a prophet like you from among their brethren; and I will put my words in his mouth, and he shall speak to them all that I command him" (Deut. 18:18). The meaning of both verses is the same—that God will see to it that there are always prophets who, like Moses, will proclaim God's sovereign will to the people.

We naturally ask how closely the picture given in Deuteronomy 18:18 corresponds to the facts as they are set before us in the Old Testament. At once we may think of the prophet Samuel, who exercised authority in the central shrine at Shiloh (1 Sam. 3:20), or of Elijah and Elisha, the center of whose activity seems to have been at the ancient Israelite sanctuaries of Gilgal and Shechem. These men, like Moses, proclaim the law of God, and amid the general disintegration of the life of Israel strive for the establishment of a concrete, contemporary sovereignty of God over his people. Thus Elijah resists the claim of King Ahab to unlimited political and dynastic supremacy, condemns the murderous cupidity of the rulers (1 Kings 21), and overthrows the priests of Baal, whose influence had been becoming increasingly dominant (1 Kings 18). Against all tendencies to assimilation and confusion (1 Kings 18:21), Elijah proclaims that the LORD alone is God and Lord: "The LORD, he is God; the LORD, he is God" (1 Kings 18:39).

In the ancient sanctuaries, in contrast to the state sanctuaries, Israel's earlier tradition of religious worship was

45

still alive. They were still the source and center of a certain prophetic power. But in course of time even these sanctuaries fell under the spell of Canaanitish heathenism. The prophets of the eighth century B.C., above all Amos and Hosea, came *from outside* to the state sanctuaries, the inner life of which had become corrupted. Thus we can picture Amos standing by the side of the traditional Pilgrim's Way of Israel and crying aloud the terrifying words: "Come to Bethel, and transgress; to Gilgal, and multiply transgression; bring your sacrifices every morning, your tithes every three days; offer a sacrifice of thanksgiving of that which is leavened, and proclaim freewill offerings, publish them; for so you love to do, O people of Israel! says the Lord GOD" (Amos 4:4–5).

Now the prophets stand aloof from the official sanctuaries, and warn the people against having recourse to the traditional holy places: "Do not seek Bethel, and do not enter into Gilgal or cross over to Beer-sheba" (Amos 5:5). To take part in the worship of this people that has fallen away from the LORD is itself sinful. The altars themselves serve no purpose but that of sinning (Hos. 8:11).

Whence come these prophets, who suddenly swoop down like eagles, who stand aloof from the official sanctuaries and yet proclaim the word of the LORD? Amos tells us that God "took me from following the flock," and commissioned him as a prophet and sent him forth (Amos 7:10–17). So, while Israel imagines that it has the LORD near at hand and under its control in the sanctuaries, the same LORD manifests his freedom by approaching the people from a completely different direction. These prophets of the Old Testament, who stand aloof from the official

46

worship, are witnesses to the freedom of Jehovah and to his unbroken sovereignty over his people. Hosea unmistakably stands in that line of prophets which, in Deuteronomy 18:18, is spoken of as starting with Moses and as following in succession to him. Hosea himself speaks of Moses as a prophet (Hos. 12:13), and is aware that the LORD has spoken to his people from time to time through prophets (Hos. 6:5; 9:8; 12:10). He regards his own ministry as a continuation of the line of this regular prophetic witness. The only difference is that he has nothing to do with the great sanctuaries; he comes to deliver his message to Israel in that free independence in which God also exercises his sovereignty in a time of which the characteristic is general religious decay.

These prophets are witnesses to, and messengers of, the sovereignty of God and of the law of God. They are not the bearers of any new or revolutionary teaching. All that happens is that the old phrases of the law of God are made immediately relevant to contemporary situations. This is emphasized by Micah: "He has showed you, O man, what is good; and what does the LORD require of you but to do justice, and to love kindness, and to walk humbly with your God?" (Mic. 6:8). Yes, Israel knows quite well what the LORD demands; all that the prophet has to do is to remind them of it. But the people of God remain obstinately in a state of terrible blindness: "There is no faithfulness or kindness, and no knowledge of God in the land" (Hos. 4:1). All the principles, all the ordinances, by which the life of the people of God was to be ruled are disregarded and despised. Israel's apostasy from the sovereignty of God has brought it to such depths of delusion that cure seems now impossible. "The ox knows

47

its owner, and the ass its master's crib; but Israel does not know, my people does not understand" (Isa. 1:3). This state of ignorance and of alienation is all the more perilous in that Israel still resolutely claims as its own the name of the LORD, but is in truth wholly ignorant of the living, sovereign God. God and idols, the will of God and the desires of men, good and evil have all been ground down together into a kind of religious pulp. So it has come about that the radiant majesty of the LORD has been hidden by a covering of black darkness. Isaiah cries aloud: "Woe to those who call evil good and good evil, who put darkness for light and light for darkness, who put bitter for sweet and sweet for bitter!" (Isa. 5:20). And while the people is complacently boasting of the privilege of the covenant that it has usurped, and imagines itself to be safe in the nearness of the LORD, the message of the prophet brings the real facts of the situation to light: "They have broken my covenant" (Hos. 8:1).

It is this situation of general confusion and spiritual blindness that the prophets have to meet. They approach it directly with a characteristic type of utterance, which even in its outward form is unmistakable—denunciation, in which the guilt of the people is revealed and the basis on which they are to be judged is declared. Deeds committed against the law and the sovereignty of God are dragged out of their concealment into the light. This is what it means to be commissioned as a prophet. Micah declares: "As for me, I am filled with power, with the Spirit of the LORD, and with justice and might, to declare to Jacob his transgression and to Israel his sin" (Mic. 3:8). An example of this uncovering of the people's sin, of this placarding of it before their eyes, is to be found in the words of Isaiah: "Woe to those who join house to house, who add field to field, until there is no more room, and you are made to dwell alone in the midst of the land" (Isa. 5:8). This word of denunciation is directed against the great landed proprietors who can never be satisfied, against the rich who transgress all the principles of social order that God has appointed for his people, whose aim is to exalt themselves to the position of independent lords.

A whole collection of such denunciations could be gathered from the books of the Old Testament prophets. The prophetic word touches every aspect of life. The prophet does not recognize the existence of private or political spheres, which follow their own inherent laws and are therefore exempt from subjection to the law of God. Stern warnings are directed also to those who are at ease and to those who feel secure (Amos 6:1). But it is above all in the spheres of worship and of political life that the word of the prophet is spoken with biting sharpness. For here, more than anywhere else, man's lust for power most obstinately maintains itself under the mask of every kind of piety and expediency.

In the midst of this worship, which the pious love and the responsible leaders of the people most carefully maintain, the word of the prophet explodes like a bomb: "I hate, I despise your feasts, and I take no delight in your solemn assemblies. Even though you offer me your burnt offerings and cereal offerings, I will not accept them, and the peace offerings of your fatted beasts I will not look upon. Take away from me the noise of your songs; to the melody of your harps I will not listen" (Amos 5:21–23). This is God's emphatic "No" to the whole of this religious activity. Israel has not been called and chosen in order that he should draw near to his God with all this multitude of religious ceremonies. The word of Amos is: "Let justice roll down like waters, and righteousness like an ever-flowing stream" (Amos 5:24). Justice and righteousness—these are the foundations, the basic ordinances for the life of Israel. In these two words, justice and righteousness, the central message of the whole of Old Testament prophecy is summed up. Israel has been chosen to live according to the law of God, that is to say, to live under the sovereignty of God, a sovereignty that is intended to cover every aspect of the whole of life. Righteousness means, further, that behavior in accordance with the covenant relationship to God, through which the people brings to visible expression the fact that it is the special and chosen people of the LORD.

But the prophet's denunciation of the people is not limited to the field of worship. It extends also to their political undertakings. In the time of Isaiah, Judah was engaged in trying to enter into alliance with the Egyptian empire. From the political point of view this might be regarded as the necessary and self-evidently right policy for Judah. But the prophet exposes it in all the full gravity of its significance: "Woe to the rebellious children, says the LORD, who carry out a plan, but not mine; and who make a league, but not of my spirit, that they may add sin to sin; who set out to go down to Egypt, without asking for my counsel, to take refuge in the protection of Pharaoh, and to seek shelter in the shadow of Egypt!" (Isa. 30:1–2). *If the people of God act without reference to the will and to the counsel of the LORD, then they can only be sinful in all that they do.* In a word, these denunciations make it clear that the people of God is in practice living and acting without God; their manifold transgressions are laid bare in the words of those who speak as the commissioned representatives of the sovereignty of God.

But what is the destiny toward which these denunciations point? Prophecy is closely linked with those catastrophes which are already beginning to loom above the horizon of history. Amos and Hosea see the Assyrians approaching ever nearer. Northern Israel is overrun by the armies of the aliens and carried away into captivity. *The* LORD *is not the Lord of Israel only; he is also the Lord of history. He summons other nations to carry out his judgment on his apostate, disobedient people.* But in every case these messages of doom pronounced by earlier prophets look beyond the limits of a merely historical event. The Assyrian invasion is more than a merely historical disaster. It is God himself who is bringing on his people a judgment from which it is impossible to escape. It is true of course that the cry "Seek the LORD" rings through Amos' message of judgment, as a last appeal to the people to seek their salvation. But no man finds the way. The end comes nearer and nearer. God comes to his own people as an enemy, and sternly and implacably rejects all half-measures of repentance (Hosea 6:1–4). So the hour is drawing nearer of which Amos has said, ". . . shatter them on the heads of all the people; and what are left of them I will slay with the sword; not one of them shall flee away, not one of them shall escape" (Amos 9:1). In judgment God makes plain to Israel the worth of that gracious sovereignty which he has despised. To his people, which has presumed upon the privilege of

51

its election, he makes known his sovereign freedom—by destroying his own people.

These prophetic words are not simply human words of warning; they are words of divine power. This word of God that has been committed to the prophet falls heavy as a stone upon the earth and breaks through every human sense of security. Isaiah says, "The Lord has sent a word against Jacob, and it will light upon Israel" (Isa. 9:8). The prophetic word is not sound and nothing more; it accomplishes something, and goes forth to the thing for which it has been sent (Isa. 55:10–11). Hosea goes so far as to say that the word of the prophets hews the people of God and slays them. As the mason hews and shapes a block of stone so that it can be fitted as a squared stone into a building, so the LORD with the word of the prophet cuts and shapes poor unruly angular Israel, and cuts off those who obstinately resist his sovereignty. *Thus the prophets' announcement of judgment is not something that is to be fulfilled in a far-distant future; the word itself is already the accomplishment of judgment. It is the incomparable power with which the LORD sets history in motion, fashions it, and guides it to its predestined end.*

One further observation is required in conclusion. We must ask what the meaning and the purpose of this prophetic declaration of judgment can be. Amos, speaking in the name of God, tells us: "You only have I known of all the families of the earth; *therefore* I will punish you for all your iniquities" (Amos 3:2). It follows that when God approaches Israel in denunciation and judgment, this also is evidence of the election of this people. In other words: *the wrath of God expressed in judgment is also*

a manifestation of his love. The LORD does not abandon
the work that he has begun to do in Israel. He is still the
sovereign of his people, and in judgment is still manifest-
ing the freedom of his grace.

chapter **6**

The Judgment and the End

THE PROPHETS Amos and Hosea proclaimed their message of judgment in the northern kingdom of Israel. What they foretold came to pass within a very few years. As early as 740 B.C. the Assyrian advance toward the Mediterranean began. The conquest of northern Syria followed without delay. Israel was compelled to pay tribute, but again and again tried to break free from this oppressive state of dependence. An hour of destiny struck when Rezin, king of Syria-Damascas, gathered together a great anti-Assyrian coalition. Israel saw its last chance of escape in participation in this desperate adventure. Judah alone held aloof and refused to join the confederation.

How helplessly the people of God had become caught in the net of political ambitions is made all too plain by the events of the Syrian-Israelite war of 733 B.C. A joint army of Syrians and Israelites invaded Judah in order to compel King Ahaz to take part in the campaign against the Assyrians. Anxiety and uncertainty prevailed in the city of Jerusalem, which had now for the first time found itself drawn into the activities of war. In this time of bitter

54

need the prophet Isaiah says to the king of Judah: "Take heed, be quiet, do not fear, and do not let your heart be faint because of these two smoldering stumps of fire-brands, at the fierce anger of Rezin and Syria and the son of Remaliah" (Isa. 7:4). The summons to the king reaches its climax in the words: "If you will not believe, surely you shall not be established" (Isa. 7:9).

So, in the midst of this great crisis, a decisive word is spoken as to the line of conduct that Judah should follow. The people of God can take refuge in the LORD alone and can entrust its existence wholly to him. But, instead of hearkening, Ahaz took the Assyrians as his refuge and was constrained to bow before this great power of the heathen world. In 722 B.C. Samaria, the capital city of the northern kingdom which had been founded by Omri, was captured and destroyed. Now only the little southern kingdom of Judah is left. It had hastened to bow before the might of the Assyrian king and had agreed to bear the burden of tribute. The people of God is in danger of being wholly crushed by the political powers. Judah has clearly seen that the anti-Assyrian coalition has ended only in disaster; yet, for all that, an alliance is made with Egypt, in the hope of escaping from the burden of tribute. Trust in the powers of this world is still the last hand-hold, which the people will not let go. But the prophet Isaiah tells them plainly that Assyria has been raised up as an instrument of the wrath of God, to carry out his sentence on ungodly Judah (Isa. 10).

Judah failed to take warning from the fate of the northern Israel. Although King Hezekiah made an earnest attempt to bring about a reformation of the life of the people (2 Kings 18:3 ff.), it was not long before that process of the total disintegration of political, social, and religious life, which had long been at work in Judah also, began to take effect again. No blow, no disaster, avails to awaken the people from their godless indolence. The prophet Isaiah asks his people: "Why will you still be smitten, that you continue to rebel? The whole head is sick, and the whole heart faint. From the sole of the foot even to the head, there is no soundness in it" (Isa. 1: 5–6). The root of all the evil lies in the fact that the worship at Jerusalem is characterized by religious and moral decay. Behind the sacrifices hides a heart that is unalterably inclined to wickedness (Isa. 1:10–17).

It is of course undeniably true that extensive religious activity and a deep devotion to the sanctuary have left their mark on every part of the people's life; and yet the stern judgment of Isaiah is true: "Because this people draw near with their mouth and honor me with their lips, while their hearts are far from me, and their fear of me is a commandment of men learned by rote; therefore, behold, I will again do marvelous things with this people, wonderful and marvelous, and the wisdom of their wise men shall perish, and the discernment of their discerning men shall be hid" (Isa. 29:13–14). The whole religious life in Jerusalem is formal and empty. With their lips the worshipers call on the LORD, and pronounce the name of the God of Israel; but the heart, the center of all thought and action, is not touched by belief in the sovereignty of God. So Judah too is ripe for the judgment and the end. God's people are not prepared to make the venture of total dependence on God.

At the end of the eighth century B.C., the Judean state, so deeply involved in political adventures, is threatened by the Assyrians. Jerusalem is besieged. "Your country lies desolate, your cities are burned with fire; in your very presence aliens devour your land; it is desolate, as overthrown by aliens. And the daughter of Zion is left like a booth in a vineyard, like a lodge in a cucumber field, like a besieged city" (Isa. 1:7–8). But the time has not yet come when those disasters, which have already fallen upon the northern kingdom, are to fall upon Jerusalem and Judah as well.

The most notable feature of the first years of the seventh century B.C. was the activities of the ungodly King Manasseh. He had submitted to the king of Assyria as his vassal. In consequence, he was required to introduce the heathen official worship into the very Temple itself, and so to let a flood of abominable Canaanitish rites and customs pour in upon the life of the people. Yet even in this time of the very deepest corruption great things were in preparation. In deep secrecy the way was being made ready for a last comprehensive attempt at a renewal of the life of Israel.

The star of the Assyrian world-empire sank. The young King Josiah was enthroned in Jerusalem. Then came the appointed moment for this great movement of renewal. What has come to be known as the "Deuteronomic group" had collected the old traditions of the law of Israel and had written them down. A copy of this writing was found in the Temple and was brought to King Josiah (2 Kings 22). Under its influence Josiah solemnly proclaims a comprehensive reform of the life of the people in church and state. Alien forms of worship and foreign practices which had intruded into the sanctuary of God are removed. The outward signs of the Canaanitish fertility cult are blotted

57

out (2 Kings 23:4 ff.). The climax of the great reform, however, is the public reading of the law of God, and the solemn entry of the people upon a covenant relationship with God. Old and young alike pledge themselves to serve the LORD with all their heart and with all their soul (2 Kings 23:1–3). What Josiah was doing, at this late hour in history, was to lay afresh the liturgical foundations of the life of the confederation of the twelve tribes of Israel. For the proclamation of the law of God and the pledge made by the assembled people to observe the covenant of God were ancient usages at the central sanctuaries of Israel. Thus, after many years of inward and outward decay, the sovereignty of God is once more visibly apparent in all its splendor.

In this time of the decay of the Assyrian power, the state of Judah succeeded in extending its territories and in strengthening the ordering of its national life. Many of the Jews may have been dreaming of a restoration of the ancient empire of David. But this dream of national and political greatness, which accompanied the wave of religious renewal, was soon to be followed by a terrible awakening. Josiah opposed the advance of the Egyptian Pharaoh Necho, and fell in battle at Megiddo (605 B.C.). Overnight all the hopes of Judah fell to the ground. Furthermore, it quickly became clear that the great reform of Josiah had resulted not in an inner renewal of religion, but only in an outward restoration. The years of rapid recovery had been marked not so much by a desire of the people to submit once again to the sovereignty of their God, as by a longing for a religious and national restoration of the kingdom of Israel.

The prophet Jeremiah looks back on the whole road

that the people of God had traveled; and the result is a deeply disturbing estimate of the spiritual penury into which Israel has now fallen. How was it in the beginning, in the early days? Then Israel loved its God and followed him (Jer. 2:2). Then Israel was a holy people, taken up by the LORD into a covenant relationship with himself (Jer. 2:3). But all too soon Israel turned away from God, followed after vanities, and itself became ever increasingly worthless (Jer. 2:5). However, the real fault of Israel, according to the judgment of Jeremiah, lay in this—that in all the many and rapidly changing situations through which it had passed in the course of its history it had failed to ask the urgently important question: "Where is the LORD?" (Jer. 2:6). Even the priests had not asked, "Where is the LORD?" (Jer. 2:8). All of them had foolishly allowed themselves to be beguiled by those new foreign deities whom Israel had encountered on its journey. Jeremiah's utterance reaches its climax in the words: "My people have committed two evils: they have forsaken me, the fountain of living waters, and hewed out cisterns for themselves, broken cisterns, that can hold no water" (Jer. 2:13). A little later God addresses the people directly in the words: "Why do you complain against me? You have all rebelled against me, says the LORD" (Jer. 2:29).

Even in this last hour the wooing, enticing words of the prophetic invitation ring out yet once more: "Return, faithless Israel, says the LORD. I will not look on you in anger, for I am merciful, says the LORD; I will not be angry for ever. Only acknowledge your guilt, that you rebelled against the LORD your God and scattered your favors among strangers under every green tree, and that you have not obeyed my voice, says the LORD" (Jer. 3: 12–13).

But here too the summons to repentance beats in vain against a dead wall of self-confidence and hardness of heart. In Judah the word is passed round from mouth to mouth: "He will do nothing; no evil will come upon us, nor shall we see sword or famine. The prophets will become wind; the word is not in them" (Jer. 5:12–13). In tones of incantation the inhabitants of Jerusalem point to the presence of the Temple in their midst (Jer. 7:4). The idea that the LORD could give his own chosen sanctuary over to destruction seems to them quite incredible! This religious self-confidence is enhanced by the false prophets, who lightheartedly set themselves to charm away with a conventional message of deliverance the disasters that have come upon the people (Jer. 8:11). On the very brink of the coming destruction Jeremiah has to enter into controversy with these false prophets. The LORD has not sent them; and yet they come before their hearers with the claim that they are bearers of the word of God (Jer. 23:21). All that they are really proclaiming are the dreams and the wishful thinking of their own fanatical hearts (Jer. 23:28–29). The outstanding difference, however, between Jeremiah and the false prophets is that these messengers of deliverance unvaryingly proclaim the protective nearness of God, whereas Jeremiah is concerned to make clear to this overconfident people that the LORD is a God who works "afar off" (Jer. 23:23). Once again, as in northern Israel, the question is this: Is God an idol, always near at hand, who can be conjured up by magical incantations to save his people? Or is he the free, remote sovereign of his people?

60

Jeremiah's declarations of judgment have struck home. In two violent assaults Judah and Jerusalem have been taken captive and destroyed. The ruling class has been carried away into exile, into imprisonment in Babylon. It is almost incomprehensible. The beginnings of Israel's history had been so full of promise; and yet the end has been judgment and overthrow. In the Old Testament there is no upward line of progress, no emergence of a religious idea; there is a steady recurrence of failure and transgression. At last, amid the ruins of the Temple and the downfall of all its religious splendor, Israel is ready to make the admission: "The LORD is in the right, for I have rebelled against his word" (Lam. 1:18). In the midst of death and destruction the people of God admits that its God was right. First it was necessary that the splendor of Israel should be cast down from heaven to earth (Lam. 2:1); only then is Israel able to recognize the sovereign lordship of JHVH. Now the guilt of those deceivers, the prophets of deliverance, can no longer be concealed; in their visions all that they have seen was "falsehood and whitewash" (Lam. 2:14), but they have not exposed the iniquity of Israel. But the word of the message of God's judgment has been fulfilled. Of a truth the LORD has arisen against his people like an enemy (Lam. 2:5); he has disowned his sanctuary (Lam. 2:7), and has accomplished judgment to the end. "The LORD has done what he purposed, has carried out his threat; as he ordained long ago, he has demolished without pity" (Lam. 2:17).

Do all the ways of the people that has so roughly rejected the sovereignty of its God lead only to judgment and to destruction? Yes; that is exactly what every reader of the Old Testament is compelled to recognize—to take serious note of this bitter journey toward judgment and destruction. The word of the Old Testament unmasks the guilt of those who were incapable of living for a single instant under the gracious sovereignty of their God. The story takes hold of the reader, and sweeps him onward to the deep places of a recognition of his own guilt, the guilt that may carry him also irresistibly onward to judgment and to destruction. Any man who fails to recognize or who denies the gravity of this situation, and of the way that has led to it, has failed to grasp the truth for which the Old Testament stands.

chapter **7**

The Coming Deliverance

THE PROPHETS of Israel uttered insistent warnings
of the judgment to come; but it would be a mistake, for
that reason, to attempt to bring them all under one single
category, and to refer to them exclusively as "prophets of
judgment." If we are right in holding that the judgment
of God is also a manifestation of his faithfulness to the
people whom he has chosen, it is no longer possible to
mark a distinction between the threatened doom and the
will of God for the salvation of his people. *Even in judgment it is the will of God to bring about deliverance.*
Through death the LORD leads men to life.

Let us turn first to the message as it is to be found
in the prophet Hosea. The people of God has been given
the terrible warning that they will be carried away captive
from their own land. Yet in the very moment in which
the prophet is speaking of the deportation of Israel to
Assyria, the types and symbols through which the message
is conveyed make it impossible to regard this exile as
mere destruction. The LORD will lead his people back to
"Egypt," into the land of slavery; and into "the wilder-

ness," that area in which Israel first entered upon the covenant relationship of trust in God. The purpose of God in the exile in Assyria is to lead his people back to a new beginning of their history. The LORD himself will make a new beginning. In the Sown Land of Canaan the people has fallen under the spell of alien powers. It is only when Israel, through the judgment of the exile, has been carried far beyond the limits within which the Baalim can exercise their magic power, that the LORD can enter into a New Covenant with his people. The second chapter of the book of Hosea proclaims the new beginning of the history of Israel. The people of Israel like an unfaithful and adulterous wife has forsaken her Lord and her God; but now in the wilderness opportunity is given for a new encounter, new espousals; and that means for the making of a new covenant.

God's judgment upon Israel had declared that they are "not my people"; but now they are again to become God's own people. A new covenant is the introduction to a new history. God is making a completely fresh beginning. The first creation of his chosen people that had come to ruin will be replaced by a new creation. The new covenant, into which God will enter with Israel, will be rich with all the mystery and all the marvel of a creative new beginning.

Hosea's message of deliverance is later taken up by Jeremiah, and expressed in the words: "Behold, the days are coming, says the LORD, when I will make a new covenant with the house of Israel and the house of Judah. . . . this is the covenant which I will make with the house of Israel after those days, says the LORD: I will put my law within them, and I will write it upon their hearts; and I will be their God, and they shall be my people. And no longer shall each man teach his neighbor and each his brother, saying, 'Know the LORD,' for they shall all know me, from the least of them to the greatest, says the LORD; for I will forgive their iniquity, and I will remember their sin no more" (Jer. 31:31–34).

A covenant creates a relation of fellowship which rests on certain quite definite principles for the ordering of life. Now one thing is quite clear. The principles for the ordering of life under the new covenant (Jer. 31:31–34), which the prophet proclaims, are exactly the same as those which prevailed under the old, the first, covenant. For the new people of God, as for the old, the basis of the covenant is the unchanging will of God to be the Lord of his people. The only thing that is changed is the way in which the people makes the laws of God its own. In the past the will of God was written on tables of stone; but now God will write his law upon the hearts of men. The prophet Ezekiel proclaims God's great act of deliverance in similar terms: "A new heart I will give you, and a new spirit I will put within you; and I will take out of your flesh the heart of stone and give you a heart of flesh. And I will put my spirit within you, and cause you to walk in my statutes and be careful to observe my ordinances" (Ezek. 36:26–27). So the renewing power of God reaches to the heart. The new creation under the new covenant penetrates to the very center of human existence.

There is also in the Old Testament another line of promise, and this finds special emphasis in the message of Isaiah. We have already seen that the kingship was a dangerous source of inward and outward corruption. Very few of the kings made any attempt to imitate the life and conduct of their ancestor David. They despised the basic principles on which the kingship in Jerusalem had been founded. David had received from God the promise: "Your house and your kingdom shall be made sure for ever before me; your throne shall be established for ever" (2 Sam. 7:16). But now that the descendants of David are exercising their sovereignty independently of the sovereignty of God, it is impossible not to ask: Where is the promise of the kingdom that is to be sure for ever?

At this point Isaiah lifts up his voice and declares that God has not taken back his promise. In line with the original promise of 2 Samuel 7, Isaiah foretells the coming of a king who will bring deliverance. In Isaiah 9, boldly, and with reference to the immediate future, the coming of the Messiah is proclaimed: "For to us a child is born, to us a son is given; and the government will be upon his shoulder, and his name will be called 'Wonderful, Counselor, Mighty God, Everlasting Father, Prince of Peace.' Of the increase of his government and of peace there will be no end, upon the throne of David, and over his kingdom, to establish it, and to uphold it with justice and with righteousness from this time forth and for evermore" (Isa. 9:6–7). In Isaiah 11:1–10 there is another picture of the wondrous rule of the coming king, who is to bring deliverance. God stands to his promise. It is his will that deliverance should break forth for his people. The Messiah is the mediator of a new ordering of all things.

Later, when the succession of the kings in Jerusalem had come to a bitter end in the Babylonian captivity, another prophet, whose name is unknown to us but whose message is preserved in Isaiah 40—55, took up the same message; but here the sovereignty through which deliverance will be brought to the people is more clearly shown to be God's own sovereignty. It is not a deliverer-king of the lineage of David who will bring about the new ordering of all things, but God himself. He himself will be the King of his people: "How beautiful upon the mountains are the feet of him who brings good tidings, who publishes peace, who brings good tidings of good, who publishes salvation, who says to Zion, 'Your God reigns.' Hark, your watchmen lift up their voice, together they sing for joy; for eye to eye they see the return of the LORD to Zion. Break forth together into singing, you waste places of Jerusalem; for the LORD has comforted his people, he has redeemed Jerusalem" (Isa. 52:7–9). But in the context of these great events, this prophet sees a mediator of the covenant also at work, a mediator who as "the Servant of the LORD" is to bring near the light of new good tidings (Isa. 42:1–9), and who as the Lamb of God is to bear all the sins of the erring and insolent people. "Surely he has borne our griefs and carried our sorrows; yet we esteemed him stricken, smitten by God, and afflicted. . . . All we like sheep have gone astray; we have turned every one to his own way; and the LORD has laid on him the iniquity of us all" (Isa. 53:4–6). The proclamation of the coming future deliverance reaches its climax in this message concerning the royal sovereignty of God and the sufferings of "the Servant of the LORD."

But when will this happen, when will the day of this deliverance dawn? When will God take to himself his sovereignty, and set his people free from all their sins? When will the bright day dawn, after the long darkness of an oppressive, tormenting obscurity? It is to be noted that Old Testament prophecy never speaks of God's great act of deliverance as of something that is going to happen in a far-distant future. On the contrary, the coming future deliverance is always thought of as being already near at hand. It is already exercising its influence upon the present. *Judgment and deliverance never follow one upon the other as separate and successive phases of history. In judgment, God the deliverer is already at work.* God takes a hand in the present; he is already here, preparing his last great act of renewal. He is on the way. Already the splendor of his sovereignty falls upon the night of guilt. In the New Testament the joyful cry of the gospel of glad tidings breaks forth in the words, "The kingdom of God is at hand." But the Old Testament also is full of the sense of the already present working of the One who is yet to come.

Now we must turn back again to the history with our question. How can God's deliverance become effective as present event in the midst of this catastrophe? A message of glad tidings given through the prophet Ezekiel casts light on the darkness of this question. In chapter 37 we read that the prophet is set down in the midst of a valley full of the dry bones of the dead. What the prophet is seeing in this vision is Israel, dead and under condemnation. Then God asks the question: "Can these bones live?" (Ezek. 37:3). Here all human wisdom and all earthly capacity are utterly helpless. But God speaks to the dry bones and says: "I will cause breath to enter you, and you shall live" (37:5). Then the LORD lifts up his voice and cries: "Behold, I will open your graves, and raise you from your graves, O my people; and I will bring you home into the land of Israel" (37:12). The creative, awakening voice of God brings a dead people back to life.

68

This word, and this alone, is to be the source of Israel's life. Through death and resurrection God brings about deliverance. There is no limit to the power and to the free operation of his grace. In Deuteronomy 32:39 we read: "See now that I, even I, am he, and there is no god beside me; I kill and I make alive; I wound and I heal; and there is none that can deliver out of my hand."

chapter 8

The People of God and the Nations

WHEN God speaks to Abraham, he says: "In you all the families of the earth will be blessed" (Gen. 12:1–3). When God condescends to Abraham and Isaac and draws near to them, what he has in mind is the salvation of all the nations. The people of God is, so to say, the point of entry, which the living God has freely chosen in order to draw near to all the nations. But he chooses a way which leads through history. It is the way of a mightily effective prophetic word, which at last in Jesus Christ became flesh. Already in the history of Israel the prophetic word has announced the claim of God to sovereignty over all the peoples. Beyond the borders of Israel, within the limits of which God has taken up his dwelling and manifested his presence, the signs of a world-wide sovereignty are already shining. The Old Testament is never concerned with the propagation of one religion, or the development of a unique religious idea; its concern is with the gradual and progressive realization of the sovereignty of God over all the nations, with the coming of God to the world. But how does this coming of God to the world of the nations take place?

Let us once again consider the message of the prophet Amos. This book considers all the surrounding peoples as being already subject to the sovereignty of the God of Israel. The prophetic word proclaims the validity of the law of God for all the peoples that dwell round about the people of God in that historical area of the Middle East. The sins of Damascus, of Gaza, of Tyre, of Edom, of Ammon, and of Moab are suddenly exposed to the light of an indictment and of a condemnation that proceeds forth from God. Cruel, inhuman actions are unreservedly condemned. God reacts against the evil deeds of the nations, even though they do not know him. But they will come to know him—through the judgment which is shortly to be accomplished. *In the indictment of the nations and in the judgment upon them, the prophet proclaims the sovereignty of the God of Israel as that power by which history is controlled.* The nations of the world are not left to themselves. Their life, their actions, are not subject to indeterminate laws of destiny. From the midst of the people of God the LORD announces himself as the Lord of all the nations. From Zion, the place in which he dwells, the thunder of the voice of the judge peals forth (Amos 1:2). Thus the other nations also—as we see from the further course of the oracle of judgment in the mouth of Amos—are judged together with Israel. Together with Israel they experience the power of God in history. The only difference is that Israel, as the chosen people of God, has the privilege of being more sternly judged than the others! (Amos 3:2).

From Amos onward, Old Testament prophecy is continuously directed toward the nations. At the center stands this certainty: *The God of Israel is also the Lord of history*. Isaiah sees God in his majesty, lifted far above the earth, far removed from that haste and striving that fill the foreground of the confused political life of men: "For thus the LORD said to me: I will quietly look from my dwelling like clear heat in sunshine, like a cloud of dew in the heat of harvest" (Isa. 18:4). "I will quietly look." This verb marks the contrast between all that pulls men this way and that—the haste, the unrest, the passion of their political strivings—and the imperturbable, majestic rest of him who holds in his hands all the threads of man's being. The restless activity of the nations is presented in sharp contrast to the patient waiting of God. Human powers set themselves to bring about at once and at any cost the overthrow of the brutal world-power of Assyria. But, through the word of the prophet, the God of Israel lets it be known that he has decided not to interfere yet—even though according to all human judgment unrighteousness and deeds of violence cry aloud to heaven. The LORD is the God afar off, the God who waits; the God whom neither the nations nor Israel itself can draw in and constrain to play a part in their plans for the future of history.

In Isaiah 18:4 the prophet depicts in two astonishing similes the absolute aloofness of the God who peacefully awaits his appointed time. "Like shimmering heat in sunlight"—this describes the intolerable glare of the southern heaven at midday. Above the sun stands a glowing splendor—the myths of the nations affirm that this is the dwelling place of the highest gods. "Like a cloud of vapor in the heat of harvest"—this is a picture of those faint white cloud-forms that arise in the heaven in the rainless season, and convey the impression of infinite height. In the whole Old Testament there is hardly any other passage which conveys in such mighty fashion the supreme exaltation of God above all the historical and political life of the peoples.

Another passage from the book of the prophet Isaiah should here be noted. As the Lord of history, the LORD rules in immeasurable wisdom: "Give ear, and hear my voice; hearken, and hear my speech. Does he who plows for sowing plow continually? does he continually open and harrow his ground? When he has leveled its surface, does he not scatter dill, sow cummin, and put in wheat in rows and barley in its proper place, and spelt as the border? For he is instructed aright; his God teaches him. Dill is not threshed with a threshing sledge, nor is a cart wheel rolled over cummin; but dill is beaten out with a stick, and cummin with a rod. Does one crush bread grain? No, he does not thresh it for ever; when he drives his cart wheel over it with his horses, he does not crush it. This also comes from the LORD of hosts; he is wonderful in counsel, and excellent in wisdom" (Isa. 28:23–29).

The special lesson that is to be learned from this passage is hidden under the form of a parable. The heart of the interpretation is to be found in recognition of the fact that the work of the farmer is not monotonous and uniform, always directed to plowing and threshing. His whole enterprise is marked by admirable skill, and accurate calculation of the seasons and of the nature of the soil in his various plots of land. These human operations of the farmer are a picture, a parable, of the operations of God in the history of the nations of the earth. God's work is not monotonously uniform. It looks as though people had put to the prophet the troubled question: Where have we got to now in this operation of God in history? Is not his working, as revealed through the words of the prophets, highly monotonous? Is it to be nothing but one judgment after another upon Israel and upon the nations? Does God do nothing in history but to break down and to destroy? "No," answers the prophet. "Look at the farmer. Is he always plowing? Is he always breaking up the soil, and doing nothing more?" Far from it. When he is plowing, he is preparing for something; he is getting the field ready for a fresh sowing. And when the right moment has come, the seed is sown in the field. That is the way in which the LORD also acts. He does not go on for ever plowing the field of history, as you imagine. He is not for ever and a day the God of wrath, who like a dark power of destiny threatens and destroys. It is true that today God is plowing; but later the time of sowing will come. God's sovereignty over his people and over the nations is governance, amazingly wise, wonderful, and all directed to one purpose. *The whole sin of men is summed up in this, that they do not look with eager attention to the Lord of history and to his working.* "You did not look to him who did it, or have regard for him who planned it long ago" (Isa. 22:11).

When will all this happen? When will the end of this long period of judgment come, and Israel and the nations enter into the salvation of God? How will it come about? In Isaiah 2:2–4, the vision of the prophet is recorded in the following terms: "It shall come to pass in the latter days that the mountain of the house of the LORD shall be established as the highest of the mountains, and shall be raised above the hills; and all the nations shall flow to it, and many peoples shall come, and say: 'Come, let us go up to the mountain of the Lord, to the house of the God of Jacob; that he may teach us his ways and that we may walk in his paths.' For out of Zion shall go forth the law, and the word of the Lord from Jerusalem. He shall judge between the nations, and shall decide for many peoples; and they shall beat their swords into plowshares, and their spears into pruning hooks; nation shall not lift up sword against nation, neither shall they learn war any more" (Isa. 2:2–4).

In Israel the twelve tribes of the confederacy used to go up every year to the central sanctuary for the great festivals. Jerusalem is the place of the presence of God. Here the members of the people of God receive the law of God and the word of God. Quarrels between the tribes are settled in the central sanctuary. The prophet now sees this procedure enlarged and extended to cover the whole world of the nations. The Gentiles sing Israel's songs of pilgrimage; they stream in crowds to the place of the presence of God, in order to live under the sovereignty of the God of Israel, to receive his law and his word. And, as in Israel quarrels between the tribes were brought to peaceful settlement at the sanctuary, so now by a universal reconciliation all strife between the nations will be brought to an end. All-encompassing peace spreads itself abroad. This is the goal to which the whole history of the Old Testament looks forward.

But the world is still full of the confusions of the hostile ambitions of the nations. The people of God and the nations of the world together are involved in desperate enterprises. At this point Old Testament prophecy enters upon a phase of sharp controversy. Now the divine decree takes the form that the sovereignty will be taken away from the kings of Israel—a threat which runs directly contrary to the usual lines of the promises of deliverance in the Old Testament. This extremely offensive and incomprehensible message of Jeremiah is expressed as follows: "Thus says the LORD of hosts, the God of Israel: This is what you shall say to your masters: 'It is I who by my great power and my outstretched arm have made the earth, with the men and animals that are on the earth, and I give it to whomever it seems right to me. Now I have given all these lands into the hand of Nebuchadnezzar, the king of Babylon, my servant' " (Jer. 27:4–6). In this utterance the people of God is made subject by God himself to the might of one of the kingdoms in the world of the nations. *The old closed boundaries of Israel, within which up till this time God has made his presence known, are now finally and visibly broken through.* It is now God himself who leads the way to a profound encounter between Israel and the other nations. God's final plans of deliverance lie hidden in the depths of his judgment upon Israel. And now all the words of judgment and salvation, which God has pronounced upon the world of the nations, come together as in a focus in the message of that unknown prophet who arose at the time of the captivity in Babylon.

The message, as proclaimed by this great prophet (Isa. 40—55), takes up once again the theme of the absolute authority of God in history. "All the nations are as nothing before him, they are accounted by him as less than nothing and emptiness. To whom then will you liken God, or what likeness compare with him?" (Isa. 40:17–18). "It is he who sits above the circle of the earth, and its inhabitants are like grasshoppers; who stretches out the heavens like a curtain, and spreads them like a tent to dwell in; who brings princes to nought, and makes the rulers of the earth as nothing" (Isa. 40:22–23). The hour has come in which the LORD will cause his sovereignty to shine forth, not only before Israel, but before all the nations of the earth: "The LORD has bared his holy arm before the eyes of all the nations; and all the ends of the earth shall see the salvation of our God" (Isa. 52:10). *God reveals his sovereignty, which brings salvation, through the act of bringing Israel back from its captivity and gathering his people together.* In this final act of liberation the saving might of God is made manifest to all the world.

Yet, in spite of all these impressive evidences of it, the nations are unwilling to recognize the power of God in history, and cling obstinately to their own independence. So God calls the peoples to a trial on a world-wide scale: "Listen to me in silence, O coastlands; let the peoples renew their strength; let them approach, then let them speak; let us together draw near for judgment" (Isa. 41:1). The purpose for which this trial is staged is the demonstration of the power of God in history. There, in the presence of the assembled peoples, Israel is brought forward as witness to bear testimony to the effective operation of the word of the LORD in history: "You are my witnesses, says the LORD, and my servant whom I have chosen. . . . I, I am the LORD, and besides me there is no savior. I declared and saved and proclaimed, when there

77

was no strange god among you; and you are my witnesses, says the LORD. I am God" (Isa. 43:10–13). So, in the end, the people of God is summoned to stand as witness before all the nations of the earth.

chapter **9**

The Origins of Judaism

WHEN the independent state of Judah came to an end, God's Old Testament people were brought into a most gravely critical situation. It was not only the state, it was the people, as such, that was in imminent danger of falling apart in fragments. Yet even in exile God's calling of his people miraculously held the threatened fellowship together. The exiles deliberately maintained a barrier between the heathen and themselves, and clung tenaciously to the faith of their fathers. For the first time, during the exile in Babylon, we encounter those mysterious forces of the later Judaism, which, when everything that ordinarily makes life in community possible has been destroyed, still finds it possible to live as a community with its eyes fixed on a future goal of which it is fully assured.

If the crisis of God's Old Testament people in exile was grave, still graver was that which followed, when, through the decree of the Persian King Cyrus (538 B.C.), the restoration of the worship of God in Jerusalem was authorized and the return of the exiles permitted. What now is to be the state of affairs in Jerusalem? Within the political organization of the Persian Empire, Jerusalem is recognized as a privileged sanctuary, the center of a state which is also a church. But within this external order strong inner tensions immediately assert themselves. The return to Zion and the re-establishment of the worship of God in Jerusalem had been accepted as the miracle that is to introduce the time of deliverance. Now men were expecting the decisive manifestation of the sovereignty of God, and the revelation of the glory of the LORD before the eyes of all the nations.

For example, from the Book of Haggai we are able to picture to ourselves the glowing expectations which accompanied the reconstruction of the Temple: soon the LORD will appear, will raise up his Anointed One, and bring to its glorious consummation that history which he began long ago in Israel. To the descendant of David, a man named Zerubbabel, Haggai proclaims the messianic promise: "I am about to shake the heavens and the earth, and to overthrow the throne of kingdoms; . . . On that day, says the LORD of hosts, I will take you, O Zerubbabel my servant, the son of Shealtiel, says the LORD, and make you like a signet ring; for I have chosen you, says the LORD of hosts" (Hag. 2:21–23). Jerusalem lives at the highest pitch of expectation. In a short time God himself will come. Already a prophet is crying aloud: "Behold, the LORD has proclaimed to the end of the earth: Say to the daughter of Zion, 'Behold, your salvation comes; behold, his reward is with him, and his recompense before him.' And they shall be called The holy people, The redeemed of the LORD; and you shall be called Sought out, a city not forsaken" (Isa. 62:11–12).

But there is a hideous discord between these high expectations and the actual situation. The restoration of Jerusalem has brought much strife and contention with it. Everyone wishes as soon as possible to get back possession of his own piece of land, to build a house, and to make sure of his own livelihood (Hag. 1). Many members of the people of God have already become assimilated to the aboriginal Canaanitish inhabitants of the land. More particularly, those who remained in Palestine during the exile have made marriage alliances with the aliens. Large sections of the people have adopted heathen worship and customs. And in this distressing state of tension the pious among the people sigh ever more deeply that the expected manifestation of God has not yet taken place. We overhear this cry of despair in a highly significant passage, Isaiah 59:9–11: "We look for light, and behold, darkness, and for brightness, but we walk in gloom. We grope for the wall like the blind, we grope like those who have no eyes; we stumble at noon as in the twilight, among those in full vigor we are like dead men. We all growl like bears, we moan and moan like doves; we look for justice, but there is none; for salvation, but it is far from us." This situation of disillusionment and embitterment is characteristic of the decades after the return of the first groups of exiles. The manifestation of God has been delayed. Life consists of nothing but a daily round which is full of sin and of anxiety.

At this time some members of the people of God, who were still living in the alien surroundings of the great Empire of the East, resolved to take a hand in the affairs of Jerusalem and to effect a reformation of its life. The efforts of Ezra and Nehemiah were directed toward a strengthening and a reformation of life in Jerusalem. Both in the inward and outward aspects of its life this problematic little church-state is to be put in order. Nehemiah promotes the building of the wall. Ezra promulgates the ordinances and the laws for the direction of the inner life.

In a great public assembly all the people who had come together in Jerusalem were made to swear allegiance to the "law of Moses" (Neh. 8). The law was introduced as a standard which was to be strictly and unconditionally observed. Strict rules were drawn up to maintain the separateness of those who were pledged to the observance of the law. Mixed marriages were broken up, the people were required to separate themselves from all alien elements; strict observance of holy days and customs was introduced.

This transformation of the life of the Old Testament people of God was the foundation on which the later Judaism was to be built, and by which the whole of its future was to be determined. The eager expectation of the immediate coming of God is thrust into the background, and its place is taken by the law, which now orders the life of men. Rules for the ordering of society, such as the law concerning separation from strangers and that governing the strict observance of the Sabbath, come to play a central and dominant part. A tremendous movement sets in, in favor of minute and learned study of the letter of the sacred text, and of scrupulous observance of even the least of the commandments. Already in the Book of Ecclesiasticus (in the Apocrypha, chapter 39) we hear the praises of the godly man, who is learned in the law and faithful to it.

Attention has thus been directed away from the acts of God, in order to concentrate all the more intensively on the acts of men. It is on this perilous slope that Pharisaism develops, as the very incarnation of that form of Judaism that lives by faithfulness to the law. The Pharisee deliberately chooses to live in separation from the world, and to submit his every action however unimportant to the rule of the law. The attempt is made to develop a formula for right living in which there are no gaps. To every question that can arise out of the circumstances of life, an answer must be ready, expressed in the form of a duty that man is bound to carry out. Even more emphatically than Ezra had done, the Pharisee sets before him the aim of preparing and making ready a holy people of God through obedience to the law. Here the great revolution has been accomplished. The primary foundations of Israel's life are no longer to be the gracious word of God addressed to it in the covenant, and the eager expectation of the coming salvation. Now, in the interval between the making of the covenant and the time of the end, Israel sets itself, by its own efforts, to establish the reality of its existence as the people of God through obedience to the law. In this activity, in which man is dependent on himself alone, we see already present that power by which the later Judaism was to live.

It is sometimes maintained that the pledge of allegiance to the law taken by the people in the time of Ezra brought Judaism into existence in its extreme legal form. But this affirmation goes beyond the facts. For in this period after the exile there was undoubtedly another line of development in Israel. There were members of the church-state in Jerusalem who did not abandon the expectation of salvation in the time of the end, even when the law had become the central point in the people's life and the power through which the whole of life was to be ordered. In these circles Jeremiah's proclamation of the salvation that God will bring in, in the last days, was in a most remarkable manner combined with life in obedience to the law of God. Jeremiah had set forth God's promise that "in the last days" the LORD himself would write his law (and with the law also the power to fulfill it) in the hearts of his people (Jer. 31:31–34). It was in the light of this promise that some members of the people of God after the exile understood that law. As a result, a wonderfully free and joyful life in obedience to the law of God became possible. This comes to expression in Psalm 40: "I delight to do thy will, O my God; thy law is within my heart" (Ps. 40:8).

This attitude to the law of God can be understood only in the light of Jeremiah 31:31–34. The time of salvation has already come; the law is now no longer an oppressive, exacting burden; it is a reality that brings joy and an assurance of the near presence of God. It is evidence of the coming into existence of a new people of God "in the time of the end," when joy in doing the will of God finds such simple expression as this: "The law of the LORD is perfect, reviving the soul; the testimony of the LORD is sure, making wise the simple; the precepts of the LORD are right, rejoicing the heart; the commandment of the LORD is pure, enlightening the eyes; the fear of the LORD is clean, enduring for ever; the ordinances of the LORD are true, and righteous altogether. More to be desired are they than gold, even much fine gold; sweeter also than honey and drippings of the honeycomb" (Ps. 19:7–10). This is the manifesto of a new people of God, which lives in a new obedience. God himself has made it new, in that he has set his law within its heart.

84

So the two ways separate. One way leads to legalistic Judaism, the other to the New Testament. One way produces the godly man who lives by duty and by a strict observance of the law; the way of the new covenant (Jer. 31—34) brings into being the new people of God, which lives in joy. The choice that men must make between these two ways is sharply set forth in the New Testament in the Gospels and in the Epistles of Paul. But both—Judaism and Christianity—are already present in germ in the world of the Old Testament.

chapter **10**

The New People of God

THE New Testament ushers in the fulfillment of all those words and deeds of God, of which the Old Testament is the announcement. In Jesus Christ, God is made manifest as the Lord of his people; in him the promised Messiah of the house of David comes to rule over Israel. Through the Gospels runs the joyful message: "The kingdom of God is at hand." The Messiah now is here. In the Old Testament his coming had been announced in these words: "The Spirit of the Lord GOD is upon me, because the LORD has anointed me to bring good tidings to the afflicted; he has sent me to bind up the broken-hearted, to proclaim liberty to the captives, and the opening of the prison to those who are bound; to proclaim the year of the LORD's favor (Isa. 61:1–2). Now Jesus announces, "Today this scripture has been fulfilled in your hearing" (Luke 4:21). And in this messianic hour, in which the sovereignty of God is present in its fullness and in its fulfillment, the new people of God is called and brought into being. God himself through his mighty word is bringing into existence a new people, both from among the Jews and from among the Gentiles. But, through this fulfillment which God has wrought in the last days, the Israel of the Old Testament is brought once again into a situation of the gravest crisis. No other man had so bitter an experience of this crisis as the Apostle Paul, who had been instructed in all the wisdom of the Pharisees. His tremendous argument in Romans 9—11 is among the most important passages in the New Testament. These chapters provide us with the master key to the New Testament understanding of the people of God in the Old Testament.

At the beginning of Romans 9 it is first clearly emphasized that to the Old Testament people of God belong "the adoption of sons, and the presence of God and the covenants and the giving of the law, the worship, and the promises" (Rom. 9:4, Greek). Jesus then, in accordance with this basic choice and appointment of God, is Israel's Messiah. This mission of the Messiah means for Israel the accomplishment of that history which began with God's calling of Abraham. And precisely in this final happening, that crisis, with which ever and again the Old Testament people of God had been faced, bursts upon them once more with greater violence than ever before. On what shall Israel choose to depend? On God, who alone is the giver, or on its own inner values and achievements? Which among the Israelites is truly a child of promise and election? Which of them, proud and self-confident, takes his stand upon the privilege of being a descendant of Abraham after the flesh? In other words: Who believes and recognizes that Israel is a creation of God and nothing else? And who imagines that to be "Israel" is a privilege which carries with it certain religious duties, and which has to be made actual by that which man himself can contribute? This Either—Or, which runs through the whole of the Old Testament, faces men in the hour of fulfillment with a choice, which in its gravity goes far beyond all human will and understanding. As we have seen, the people of God in the Old Testament always manifested the inclination and the will not to live under the sovereignty of God, but to carry out and to accomplish its mission without dependence upon him. That is how it came about that in this final hour it rejected its King and drove him to his death.

With loving eagerness the Apostle asks the question, "Has God rejected his people?" (Rom. 11:1). Israel has said its final "No" to the gracious sovereignty of God. Is the consequence that God has said his final "No" to his people of the Old Testament covenant? Paul's answer is: "God has not rejected his people whom he foreknew" (Rom. 11:2). God has remained faithful to his people, even in this final and most terrible crisis. Though Israel has obstinately held fast to its idea of fulfilling its mission and its history in its own chosen way, though blind and deluded it has passed Jesus Christ by on the other side, God has yet chosen for himself certain members of his Old Testament people, who have seen and believed that God himself has now accomplished his saving work. So, below the last line of the history of the Old Testament, the words "The End" have not yet been written. Just as in Old Testament times the living God through all his judgments had again and again found the way to a new beginning, so in this last judgment through the manifestation of his Son he has made known his grace to some among the Israelites. But, in this last crisis of Israel, the boundaries of the people of God in the Old Testament have been finally broken through. Those events, which had been foretold in the time of the exile in Babylon, have now come to fulfillment: "Through their trespass salvation has come to the Gentiles" (Rom. 11:11). Jesus calls and gathers the new people of God in the time of the end from among both Jews and Gentiles. Jesus Christ is the foundation stone of a new act of God which will embrace the whole world. He is the chief cornerstone of the new people of God (Eph. 2:14–20). The form of address which was once appropriate to the Israel of the Old Testament is now appropriate to the new people of God: "You are a chosen race, a royal priesthood, a holy nation, God's own people, that you may declare the wonderful deeds of him who called you out of darkness into his marvelous light. Once you were no people but now you are God's people; once you had not received mercy but now you have received mercy" (1 Pet. 2:9–10).

But this new people of God, which lives under the sovereignty of Jesus Christ, has quite definite principles and bases for its life; and to these Paul draws attention in the parable of the olive tree (Rom. 11:17–24). From the trunk of the holy tree of the Old Testament Israel some branches had been broken off: and the Gentiles, shoots of a wild, alien tree, have been grafted into the trunk of the holy tree. But this makes it perfectly clear that the Church of Jesus Christ lives from the root and the trunk of the Old Testament Israel. *The new people of God cannot live otherwise than on the basis of the Old Testament.* If the church came to reject the Old Testament, it would wither. In that case the Christ, in whom that church continued to confess its faith, would no longer be the

89

Anointed One of God—he would be nothing more than a religious hero. It is only when the church lives constantly on the basis of the Old Testament message of judgment and of grace that it can really live at all. Ever and again it must follow the direction given by the Apostle: "Note then the kindness and the severity of God: severity toward those who have fallen, but God's kindness to you, provided you continue in his kindness; otherwise you too will be cut off" (Rom. 11:22).

As we follow this direction of the Apostle, all that we have set forth in this book about the people of God in the Old Testament takes on a burning contemporary relevance for the Church of Jesus Christ. If the church, disregarding the warning of the Old Testament, sets out to follow its own way and to accomplish its mission in its own way, the judgment which fell upon Israel in the Old Testament will be repeated in the case of the church; the church will be cut off from the tree of election. If the Church of Jesus Christ takes the words of the Apostle seriously, it cannot but be alarmed to note that from the first century onward it has always shown an inclination to separate itself from the Israel of the Old Testament.

It has adopted Greek and Gentile ways of thinking and standards of value. It has desired to live as though its roots were in those vital powers that expressed themselves in the national and political life of the nations in the world of the heathen civilizations. Hence it has been threatened by a deadly peril, of which the church itself has for the most part been, and still is, wholly unaware.

Today the new people of God in all the world is living in just such a situation of crisis as that with which Israel of old had to wrestle when Jesus Christ came into the world. Paul ends his exposition of the problem of Israel in Romans 9—11 with a mysterious glance at the history of the new people of God in the time of the end: "Lest you be wise in your own conceits, I want you to understand this mystery, brethren: a hardening has come upon part of Israel, until the full number of the Gentiles come in, and so all Israel will be saved; as it is written, The Deliverer will come from Zion, he will banish ungodliness from Jacob; and this will be my covenant with them when I take away their sins" (Rom. 11:25–27). Here it is not stated simply that individual, specially favored members of the Old Testament Israel will again live from the root of election and in the holy tree; the promise is that when God's invitation to join the new people of God has gone out to all the nations, then "Israel as a whole" will once again be grafted into the holy olive tree. "For the gifts and the call of God are irrevocable" (Rom. 11:29). God will bring the work which he began in Abraham to a wonderful conclusion, and by this act he will reveal himself as the sovereign Lord of all the life of man in history.

When this accomplishment of the work of God comes to pass, the Gentile members of the new people of God will be thrown into a state of grave crisis. *Are we to think that this crisis has already begun?*

Something new has happened in history. In Palestine the state of Israel has been founded, and more than a million Jews have come to live there. These events should serve as a violent challenge to every single Christian in the world. Can we set any limits to what God in his sovereign love might cause to come to pass, through this alarming gathering together of the Jews in Palestine?

Whatever judgment we may be inclined to pass on

them, these events in history today ought to drive the new people of God back to consider the roots of its own existence, and to take careful note of its own origins in the Old Testament. Only if it does so will the Church of Jesus Christ learn to live not by certain religious convictions intellectually held, but in life and action to bear testimony before all the world to the reality of its election by the God who is the Lord of history, and to raise to him the hymn of praise:

> O the depth of the riches and wisdom and knowledge of God! How unsearchable are his judgments and how inscrutable his ways!
>
> For who has known the mind of the Lord, or who has been his counselor?
>
> Or who has given a gift to him that he might be repaid?
>
> For from him and through him and to him are all things. To him be glory forever. Amen.
>
> (Romans 11:33–36)